A HOME IN THE BIOME

At Home in the
DESERT

Louise and Richard Spilsbury

PowerKiDS press
New York

Published in 2016 by **The Rosen Publishing Group**
29 East 21st Street, New York, NY 10010

Produced for Rosen by Calcium
Editors: Sarah Eason and Amanda Learmonth
Designers: Paul Myerscough and Emma DeBanks

Picture credits: Cover: Shutterstock: Chantelle Bosch; Insides: Dreamstime: Valentin Armianu 4–5, Etwin Aslander 1, 9, Ddvinyl 17, Roger de Montfort 19, Michael Elliott 29, Tero Hakala 16–17, Holger Karius 20–21, Kcmatt 22–23, Mopane 21, Christian Musat 13, Michael Pettigrew 11, Pixy2000 23, Tim Roberts 28–29, Nico Smit 27, Stuart456 15; Shutterstock: Ferderic B 12–13, bikeriderlondon 7, Jim David 6–7, Dominique de La Croix 8–9, Arno Dietz 18–19, EcoPrint 24–25, Davide Guidolin 26–27, Laborant 5, Dmitry Pichugin 14–15, Sergei25 25, veleknez 10–11.

Cataloging-in-Publication Data
Spilsbury, Louise.
At home in the desert / by Louise and Richard Spilsbury.
p. cm. — (A home in the biome)
Includes index.
ISBN 978-1-5081-4560-8 (pbk.)
ISBN 978-1-5081-4561-5 (6-pack)
ISBN 978-1-5081-4572-1 (library binding)
1. Desert biology — Juvenile literature. 2. Desert ecology — Juvenile literature.
3. Desert animals — Juvenile literature. I. Spilsbury, Louise. II. Spilsbury, Richard,
1963-. III. Title.
QH541.5 S75 2016
577.54—d23

Manufactured in the United States of America

CPSIA Compliance Information: Batch BW16PK: For Further Information contact
Rosen Publishing, New York, New York at 1-800-237-9932

Contents

At Home in the Desert

Deserts are among the hottest, driest places on Earth. They are covered with sand or rocks, and get very little rain for months or even years at a time. Many deserts are burning hot during the daytime but then get freezing cold during the night. These conditions make deserts a challenging biome for plants and animals to live in. Those that are found there have some amazing adaptations to help them survive.

Desert Walking

When people think of deserts, they often think of camels. It is hard work walking across sand, so camels have wide feet to keep them from sinking in. Both sides of a camel's top lip can move independently of the other, so the animal can eat the shortest grass. The lips are so tough the camel can eat prickly plant parts, such as thorns.

People used to think camels stored water in their humps. In fact, they store food in the form of fat in the strange bumps on their backs. When they cannot find enough food, they feed on some of the fat from their humps instead. The size of the humps change depending on how much the camels have to eat, and they can last several months without food if necessary.

Camels have two rows of very long eyelashes to keep sand out of their eyes. They can even close their nostrils to keep sand out, too.

Saguaro Cacti

These famous desert plants grow branches that point upward toward the sky. They also grow very tall, very slowly. They can reach heights of 60 feet (18 m) tall and they live for up to 200 years.

Plants Without Leaves

One of the first things people notice about saguaro cactus plants, or cacti, is that they do not have leaves. This is because leaves lose water, and in the baking hot desert, no plant can risk losing water. So, cacti use their thick green stems for **photosynthesis**. They take in **carbon dioxide** from the air and mix it with water to make food using **energy** from the sun.

Cacti are covered in sharp spines. Animals that might try to eat the cacti's stems to get at their water are prevented from doing so by the sharp spines.

HOME SWEET HOME

Saguaro cacti have one very long **root** that holds them in the ground. They have other roots that grow just below the ground so they can **absorb** any rain as it soaks into the surface. These roots can spread out as wide as the saguaros are tall! Saguaro stems are **pleated**. The cacti soak up as much water as they can and the pleats **expand** to store it all.

Desert Flowers

Some plants survive in the desert by growing and dying back in one short season, before the weather gets too hot and dry.

Springing into Life

When rain falls in the desert, some flowering plants immediately start to grow, to take advantage of the water. Their stems and flowers reach above the surface in a short time. These plants do not live long, so their flowers quickly produce a lot of small, hard seeds. When the flowers die, the seeds fall and sink into the ground. They stay in the ground until the next rains fall, then the seeds burst into life.

This flowering plant, called argyroderma, *looks like a pebble for most of the year, until it flowers. This disguise helps it hide from hungry desert animals that would otherwise eat it.*

HOME SWEET HOME

Some flowering plants use a very sneaky trick to survive. *Argyroderma* is an unusual desert plant that looks like a pebble. The plant grows in clumps and it is almost impossible to identify it among the pebbles on the desert ground. In fact, it is only easy to spot this plant when rains fall and, suddenly, a pretty, brightly colored flower grows from one of the "rocks!"

Termites

Termites are small, ant-like insects that live together in groups called colonies. In each colony there are different types of termites with different jobs to do.

Workers and Soldiers

Most termites are worker termites that find and collect plants to eat and build nests. Desert termites build nests called mounds out of a mixture of soil, termite spit, and dung. Soldier termites have unusually shaped heads with large jaws. It is their job to look after the nest where the colony lives and attack intruders.

Termite mound walls have a lot of tiny holes to let in air from outside. They also contain many rooms that are connected by tunnels. Termites use the rooms to store food and grow tiny areas of **fungus** to feed on. The rooms also house eggs laid by the large queen termite, which grow into new termites. Termites spend most of their time in a nest found just below the ground, under the mound.

A termite mound can take 5 years to build and can be up to 17 feet (5 m) tall, or higher. Heavy rains and attacks by animals that eat termites damage the mound. If this happens, worker termites busily carry mouthfuls of dirt to fill in the holes and mend their home.

Fennec Foxes

Fennec foxes are the smallest foxes in the world. They measure about 15 inches (38 cm) long, with an 8-inch (20 cm) tail. The fox's most striking feature is its huge ears. These can be half the length of the fox's body!

Supersmart Ears

The fox's big ears are incredibly useful in the desert. They allow the animal to hear **prey** such as insects and snails moving around underground. The ears also have more **blood vessels** per square inch than any other part of the body. These vessels are just below the surface of the skin. As blood passes through them, heat from the blood escapes into the air. This helps keep the fox from overheating in the sun.

When the fennec fox is not hunting for food, it snuggles up with its family in its long underground burrow.

HOME SWEET HOME

Fennec foxes have a coat of thick, sandy-colored fur that protects them from the sun and keeps them warm at night. The pale color helps the foxes blend in with their sandy biome, and absorbs less heat than dark fur. There is even fur around the foxes' paw pads, to protect them from the hot sand and help them grip the sandy ground.

13

Meerkats

Meerkats have striped brown fur that helps them blend in with the sandy soil where they live. This makes it difficult for predators to spot them. Meerkats live in groups. While some meerkats in the group feed, others take turns as guards.

Keeping Lookout

Guard meerkats stand up tall on their back legs or climb a rock or tree to keep a lookout for predators such as eagles in the sky, or wild dogs or snakes on the ground. If guards spot a predator, they make a loud barking sound and all the meerkats run for their burrow.

The dark patches of fur around a meerkat's eyes make it look like it is wearing sunglasses! These black patches reduce the glare from bright sunlight and help the meerkat see far away. This helps the animal keep watch for danger.

HOME SWEET HOME

Meerkats use their powerful claws to dig burrows. Their ears fold back to keep out the dirt as they dig. Meerkats stay in their burrows at night and come out in the daytime to find food. They sniff the air, and if they smell an insect, they turn over stones or dig into the ground to find it. They return to their burrows in the middle of the day, when the sun is strongest.

Kangaroos

Red kangaroos live in the wide open spaces of Australia's deserts. They travel long distances every day by hopping quickly on their large and powerful back legs. They can bounce along at speeds of about 30 miles per hour (50 kph). Hopping is a great way to get around in the desert because it helps kangaroos save energy in the sapping heat.

Life in the Desert

Kangaroos are well-adapted for life in the desert. They have big ears to help them hear sounds across the open space. They get most of the water they need from the grasses and leaves they eat, although they also drink from pools of water when they find them. They have large front teeth for chopping off pieces of plants, and large flat teeth at the back of their mouths for grinding up tough plants.

The kangaroo's huge tail helps it balance when it is hopping along, but it is so long and heavy that it makes walking slower.

HOME SWEET HOME

To keep cool, a kangaroo pants a little like a dog and licks its arms. When the spit on its arms dries in the sun and wind, it helps cool the animal's body.

Sidewinders

Sidewinder snakes are named for their unusual way of moving. They are covered in rough scales that grip the sand as they travel. To move, the snake throws its head forward and then the rest of its body catches up. This looping movement means that only two parts of the body ever touch the hot sand. A sidewinder moves very quickly, leaving a series of S or J patterns in the sand.

Out at Night

The sidewinder is **nocturnal**, and it feeds on **rodents**, lizards, and birds. In the darkness, it uses body parts on its head, called heat pits, to sense the warmth from small animals. To catch a meal, the snake injects powerful **venom** into its prey. It then follows the animal until it dies, and eats it. When it is very hot or cold, a sidewinder rests inside other animals' burrows or in spaces between rocks.

HOME SWEET HOME

Sidewinders are also known as horned vipers because the snakes seem to have horns above their eyes. In fact, these horns are special scales. They keep sand from covering the sidewinder's eyes when it is buried.

Sidewinder snakes are colored to blend in with their surroundings. They often bury themselves just under the sand and wait patiently to strike small animals that pass by.

Chameleons

The desert chameleon is an odd-looking creature. It has a big, triangular head, bulging eyes that can move in different directions, and toes joined together, with two or three on each foot. It also has a very long tongue!

Looking Around

The eyes on top of the chameleon's head help it spot prey and watch out for hawks, jackals, and other predators. Its feet keep it from sinking into sand and help it dig holes to reach cooler sand below the surface. It uses its long tongue to catch insects (such as beetles), small snakes, and other prey. Its long legs help it run fast, and it can straighten them to lift its body off the hot sand. This funny movement is called "stilting."

The Namaqua chameleon's tongue can be twice as long as its body. The tongue has a sticky tip, which catches prey when it shoots out at high speed.

HOME SWEET HOME

Desert chameleons are usually gray and brown, but they can change color to survive. In the morning, when they need to warm up after a cold night, they can turn darker to absorb the heat. In the hottest part of the day, they can turn lighter to keep cool.

Tortoises

Desert tortoises are the only tortoises that can survive in burning hot deserts. Their special skill is their ability to dig burrows up to 6 feet (2 m) deep. These tortoises live in deserts that have a winter and a summer. The deserts are hot in winter, but even hotter in summer.

Sleepyhead!

It is rare to see desert tortoises because they spend so much time in their burrows. They escape there in the summer when it is very hot. In the winter, they go into a deep sleep until the spring. The burrows also hide tortoises from predators. If a tortoise is attacked outside the burrow, it pulls its head, legs, and tail under its shell for protection.

The desert tortoise uses its strong legs and thick claws to dig its underground burrow. Its front legs are protected by a covering of thick scales.

HOME SWEET HOME

Desert tortoises get almost all the water they need from the desert grasses and other plants that they eat. They also dig pits in the desert's sandy soil, which fill with rainwater. When it rains, the tortoises remember where these pits are and head over to stock up on water. They can even store water in their **bladder** and reabsorb it if they need to.

23

Ostriches

Ostriches are the biggest birds in the world. They are taller than most adult men! Ostriches have wings like other birds, but they cannot fly. Instead, they slowly walk through their biome, with their heads held high. They have eyes as big as baseballs that are constantly on the lookout for danger. If ostriches spot a predator, their long legs help them run away very quickly. Ostriches can run faster than any other bird.

Long Neck, Little Head

An ostrich has a very long neck and a small head. It bends its long neck down to the ground to eat grasses, other plants, and sometimes insects. It also eats pieces of sand and stones. These sit in the bird's stomach and help it grind up its food.

HOME SWEET HOME

Ostriches have long, fluffy feathers on their backs and wings. At night, they lie down on the ground to sleep, and wrap their wings around their bodies like blankets. This helps keep them warm when the temperature drops.

If it gets very hot, ostrich chicks can hide from the sun under the shade of their parents' large, fluffy wings.

Scorpions

Scorpions are tough creatures that hunt at night and escape the desert heat by resting in an underground burrow during the day. They have four pairs of clawed legs that help them run quickly across desert sand to chase prey or escape predators.

Pinch and Sting!

A desert scorpion has huge **pincers** at the front of its body and a large, curved tail with a stinger at the back. It uses its powerful front pincers to dig its burrow and to grab and kill insects, spiders, and other prey. A scorpion sometimes crushes prey with its pincers, or uses the pincers to hold prey still while it brings down its tail to sting it!

Scorpions have a tough outer covering that acts like armor to keep them from being crushed. It also protects them from the harsh desert sun and from the sand that is hurled against them in a sandstorm. The covering also keeps scorpions from losing too much water in the heat.

A scorpion's tail is made up of sections that allow it to easily curl over and forward. The stinger at the end of the tail injects venom that is powerful enough to kill small animals and even stun prey as large as the scorpion.

Deserts Under Threat

Many other incredible plants and animals live in desert biomes, but their homes are under threat. People take over desert land to build towns, airports, and other buildings or to dig mines for useful substances such as oil. In some places, farmers let too many farm animals eat desert plants, leaving too few for wild desert animals to eat.

Protecting Our Deserts

Around the world, people are trying to protect desert biomes. Scientists study deserts to see how plants and animals are being affected by changes. Governments protect some areas of desert so people cannot build on them or dig them up. **Conservation** groups also raise money to help protect **endangered** desert animals, such as the pronghorn antelope.

One of the reasons that the pronghorn antelope is an endangered desert animal is that people have taken over the land where it used to live.

HOME SWEET HOME

Pronghorn antelopes need to be able to travel long distances to find enough food to eat throughout the year. Today, fences, roads, and buildings break up the wide open spaces it once wandered in search of grasses and other plants to eat.

Glossary

absorb To soak up.

adaptations Changes to survive in an environment.

biome A community of plants and animals living together in a certain kind of climate.

bladder The part of an animal's body that stores urine.

blood vessels Tubes that carry blood around the body.

carbon dioxide A gas in the air we breathe. Carbon dioxide is also found in water.

conservation The act of guarding, protecting, or preserving something.

endangered When a plant or animal is in danger of dying out.

energy The power or ability to do work.

expand To grow or widen.

fungus A living thing such as mold, yeast, or a mushroom.

nocturnal To be active at night.

photosynthesis The process plants use to make their own food.

pincers A large pair of claws.

pleated Folded.

predators Animals that catch and eat other animals.

prey An animal that is caught and eaten by other animals.

rodents Animals with large front teeth for gnawing, such as mice and rats.

root A plant part that grows under the ground and takes in water.

scales Small, overlapping plates of hard material.

venom A poison that animals use to attack and kill prey.

Further Reading

Dale, Selena. *21 Strange Animals That Live In The Desert: Extraordinary Animal Photos & Fascinating Fun Facts For Kids* (Weird & Wonderful Animals). CreateSpace Independent Publishing Platform, 2015.

Hinman, Bonnie. *Keystone Species that Live in Deserts* (A Kid's Guide to Keystone Species in Nature). Hockessin, DE: Mitchell Lane Publishers, Inc., 2015.

Johansson, Philip. *The Desert: Discover This Dry Biome* (Discover the World's Biomes). New York, NY: Enslow Elementary, 2015.

Riggs, Kate. *Camels* (Amazing Animals). Mankato, MN: Creative Paperbacks, 2014.

Royston, Angela. *Desert Food Chains* (Food Chains and Webs). Mankato, MN: Heinemann-Raintree, 2015.

Websites

PowerKids Press has developed an online list of websites related to the subject of this book. This site is updated regularly. Please use this link to access the list: **www.powerkidslinks.com/ahitb/desert**

Index